CONTENTS

AUTHOR & HIS RELATIONSHIP WITH HAMBURG

INTRODUCTION

DAY 1 – AROUND THE CENTRE

DAY 2 – WATER & NIGHTLIFE

DAY 3 – TOWARDS THE WEST

GOT MORE TIME? THERE IS STILL A LOT TO SEE

THANKS VERY MUCH

Instagram: german_world_explorer87
Youtube: Sven G.B.

CONTENTS

AUTHOR & HIS RELATIONSHIP WITH HAMBURG

The author was born and raised in Southern Germany, close to Stuttgart. For almost two years he lived, worked, studied and could enjoy the beautiful city of Hamburg. To be precise, it was between 2017 and 2019. Since the author works in shipping, he inevitably fell in love with the port city. But it is not absolutely necessary to work in the same area in order to immediately like this city: It is because it is a very cosmopolitan, green, entertaining, unique city full of beautiful canals, huge parks, hidden cafes, restaurants, bars, clubs, stores, events, nationalities and much more.

***

Come with Sven and get to know Hamburg the very best way. Of course, you can't see everything in three days. The tours recommended in this travel guide have already been tested and approved by the author's many visitors during his stay. Because for some reason, Hamburg is considered one of the most beautiful cities in Germany and also one of the cities with the best quality of life in the world.

***

The author tried his best to be able to help you on your journey with this guide. Book. He really likes maps. Don't be surprised if you find many of them. The author hopes you like it and, more importantly, hopefully you have a great time in Hamburg. He likes facts more than long texts. He also loves photographs, and even though he is not a professional, he likes to take the time to take a good picture.

This guide is a mix of what was just mentioned: Maps, short but precise texts, facts and photos of the greatest places. Enjoy your stay in the amazing city of Hamburg!

INTRODUCTION

Welcome to Hamburg! The famous port city in Northern Germany. I would like to introduce you to the most important data:

Population:

Almost 2 million people live in Hamburg. According to a census from December 2019 it was exactly 1,899,160. After Berlin it is the second largest city in Germany. Thereafter come Munich, Cologne and Frankfurt.

Dimension:

Hamburg is extended over an area of 755.22 km2. As a comparison: The German capital Berlin has over twice the population of Hamburg, but is extended over an area of 891.8 km2 (just slightly larger). Munich has almost the same population (1,471,508 in December 2018), but the area is much smaller (310.7 km2). In summary, the extension of the city of Hamburg is fairly large.

Public transport:

A lot can be written about public transport here. But I would like to explain the most important. To get started, you can use three different types of public transport in Hamburg, excluding bicycles:
There is the subway (U), the trains (S) and buses. Because the bus transport is more complicated, I will only explain the subway and the trains in more detail.

Before going on either the subway, or a train, you must buy a ticket at one of the machines. There is no control or a closed area like in many other cities. However, there might be an inspector at some stage who wants to see the ticket. So you should always keep the ticket with you while using the public transport. The fine of travelling without one, is around 60 euros.

The cost of a single trip varies and depends on the distance. There are also different zones. For a traveler, the best ticket is the daily ticket. This one can be used all day from 9:00 AM to 6:00 AM the next day. The cost is 6.40 Euros per person (2020).

More information is available on the website below. And in general, there are many ticket machines at every station with several languages available.

Official website for public transport in Hamburg: https://www.hvv.de/en

Hamburg subway lines

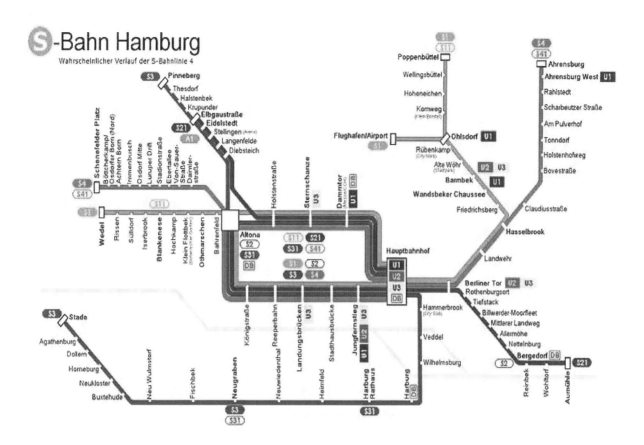

Hamburg train lines

Nationalities:

In Hamburg there are a lot of nationalities, which makes the city very much cosmopolitan. More than 30,000 Polish people live here, and over 15,000 Syrians have arrived in recent years. And for a longer time there has been a Portuguese colony with more than 10,000 people. Over 8,000 Italians and Iranians can be found. There are Spaniards and Greeks of over 7,000 each. And even from the African country Ghana alone, more than 6,000 people made it to Hamburg. Around 5,800 Filipinos have arrived from even further away.

DAY 1 – WALK AROUND THE CENTRE

	MÖNCKEBERGSTRASSE - STREET **(+/- 10 minutes)**
LOCATION / MAP	
HOW TO GET THERE?	Line U3 – Station Mönckebergstrasse
WHAT IS IT?	The "Mönckebergstraße" is one of the most famous streets of the city with their various shops and malls. It is the connection between the main train station and the famous town hall, where we'll go later.
SUGGESTIONS / INTERNET	If you are coming in December, try to walk around here in the dark, in order to see the Christmas markets and feel the special atmosphere with the lights. It is well worth seeing.
FOOD OR DRINKS?	Try a typical curry sausage in the "snack bar" "Mö Grill".

	**BINNENALSTER "LAKE"** **(+/- 30 minutes)**
LOCATION / MAP	
HOW TO GET THERE?	Lines U3 - Mönckebergstraße or Jungfernstieg U1,U2, U4, S1, S2, S3, S21 or S31
WHAT IS IT?	The "Binnenalster" looks like a small lake, but actually comes from the main river, the "Elbe". Here we recommend to take a walk around it and enjoy the beautiful views. There are many ducks and swans as well.
SUGGESTIONS / INTERNET	Bring your camera and sit on a bench to enjoy the view.
FOOD OR DRINKS?	The CIU bar offers a great view of the lake (picture above) and excellent cocktails. Especially in summer (between May and September) it is recommended. More touristy is the famous "Alex" restaurant / bar - many tables are outside where you can also enjoy the view of the "Binnenalster".

JUNGFERNSTIEG / RATHAUS "TOWN HALL" (+/- 20 minutes)

LOCATION / MAP	
HOW TO GET THERE?	Lines U3 - Rathaus or Jungfernstieg U1,U2, U4, S1, S2, S3, S21 or S31
WHAT IS IT?	After the walk, and next to the "Alex", you will be at the Jungfernstieg, where you have a chance to do a boat tour, which is highly recommended (on our second day). A 2 minutes walk from here you will reach the amazing building of the town hall. It is definitely a great symbol of the city, and also place for various festivals, such as the large Christmas market in December.
SUGGESTIONS / INTERNET	The town hall and its courtyard are freely accessible. Guided tours to the interior are offered, against a small fee. It is definitely worth it to go: https://www.hamburg.com/sights
FOOD OR DRINKS?	Daniel Wischer is an excellent restaurant whose specialty is local fish. The prices are relatively low. The bar "Parlament" is right below the town hall, and has a great atmosphere and long tradition. Also very worth it to pay a vist.

	# TROSTBRÜCKE - BRIDGE / ST NIKOLAI - MONUMENT (+/- 20 minutes)
LOCATION / MAP	
HOW TO GET THERE?	Line U3 – Rathaus
WHAT IS IT?	After we passed one of the oldest bridges "Trostbrücke" in the city we reach the monument of the church "St. Nikolai ". The remains of this church are a monument from the Second World War. Hamburg was attacked by the English and the city badly destroyed. Upstairs in the remaining tower there is a viewpoint where you can see the whole city. And in the underground below, there is a very informative museum of this July 1943 air attack.
SUGGESTIONS / INTERNET	The lift up to the viewpoint as well as the museum are not for free, but well worth it. There are discounts for Students. https://english.mahnmal-st-nikolai.de
FOOD OR DRINKS?	Cöllns is a restaurant with typical Nordic cuisine. The prices are a bit higher, but the quality is very good. Go for it, if your are hungry and want to try something typical.

KRAMERAMTSSTUBEN "PASSAGE"
(+/- 10 minutes)

LOCATION / MAP	
HOW TO GET THERE?	Line U3 – Rödingsmarkt
WHAT IS IT?	This is a place with a lot of history. The houses are not only very beautiful, but also very old (built between 1620 and 1700). These are one the few ones that have survived several fires and floodings in the city.
SUGGESTIONS / INTERNET	http://krameramtsstuben.de/
FOOD OR DRINKS?	There is a restaurant in the same place with the same name. It's a bit touristy, but the food is typical and very good.

	**PORTUGIESENVIERTEL "NEIGHBORHOOD" (+/- 15 minutes)**
LOCATION / MAP	
HOW TO GET THERE?	Line U3 - Landungsbrücken
WHAT IS IT?	Back in the 1970s, this became a popular neighborhood, where not only Portuguese, but also Spanish immigrants would meet up. It is known for its various restaurants, bars and cafes, and the Mediterranean flair.
SUGGESTIONS / INTERNET	https://www.portugiesenviertel-hamburg.de/
FOOD OR DRINKS?	Pizzeria Luigi's is one of the most famous restaurants in the entire city. It is known for its unique atmosphere/decoration, excellent pizzas and very special waiters (surprise when the bill comes). Even if you probably have to wait some time at the entrance, it's totally worth it!

	# LANDUNGSBRÜCKEN – ELBTUNNEL ## (+/- 40 minutes)
LOCATION / MAP	
HOW TO GET THERE?	Line U3 - Landungsbrücken
WHAT IS IT?	The "Landungsbrücken" are kind of a train station for the ferries, which are also part of the public transport system. But now we're not getting on a boat, we're going on a walk beneath the river. The famous tunnel "Elbtunnel" was built in 1911 and gave direct access to the port for its workers from the city. Today it is a very touristy and popular place. On the other side, after a 426 meters walk, you have a great view of the city.
SUGGESTIONS / INTERNET	https://www.hamburg.de/alter-elbtunnel/
FOOD OR DRINKS?	On the other side of the tunnel, near the viewpoint, there is a small kiosk where you can buy almost anything: a beer, beverage, sandwich, hot dog etc. In winter, a "mulled wine" is recommended, which is a hot and very popular wine, which will help you to keep warm.

	**ELBPHILHARMONIE** **(+/- 25 minutes)**
LOCATION / MAP	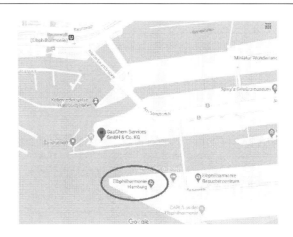
HOW TO GET THERE?	Line U3 - Baumwall
WHAT IS IT?	This building with a worldwide unique architecture has become the new icon of the city. It is a beautiful philharmonic orchestra, known for its great concerts of world famous artists. Although it's a little bit expensive it is definitely worth it to go. The entrance to the main platform is for free and there are several dining options.
SUGGESTIONS / INTERNET	https://www.elbphilharmonie.de/en/
FOOD OR DRINKS?	Störtebeker is a good restaurant/bar, where you can just come for a beer in order to enjoy the beautiful view. The prices are relatively low - (https://www.stoertebeker-eph.com/)

	**HAFENCITY "NEIGHBORHOOD" (+/- 10 minutes)**
LOCATION / MAP	
HOW TO GET THERE?	Line U4 - Überseequartier
WHAT IS IT?	It is one of the newest sectors in the city. Where in the past even dock workers lived, today one can find not only modern office buildings, but also luxurious apartments, restaurants, cafes, bars, shops and much more.
SUGGESTIONS / INTERNET	https://www.hafencity.com/en/home.html

	**SPEICHERSTADT** **(+/- 30 minutes)**
LOCATION / MAP	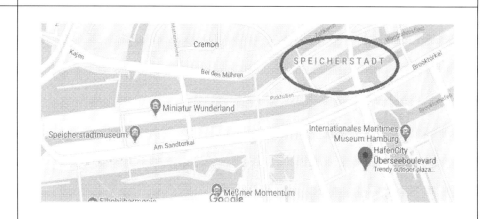
HOW TO GET THERE?	Line U1 - Messberg
WHAT IS IT?	The Speicherstadt was declared as World Heritage Site in 2015. Goods from the port used to be stored here - but today there are all sort of things: event centers, restaurants, cafes, carpet shops from the Middle East, but also apartments, offices, museums and much more.
SUGGESTIONS / INTERNET	https://www.hamburg.com/architecture/11748606/speicherstadt/
FOOD OR DRINKS?	The KAFFEERÖSTEREI is exactly what the name says in German – a coffee roaster. You can buy delicious coffee here, but also chocolate, sweets, tea etc. You can also sit down for a coffee and a delicious pice of cake. Even if there are many tables, they are often occupied. Because of the good quality, this place is always very busy.

	# MUSEUM MINIATURMUSEUM ## (at least 1 hour)
LOCATION / MAP	
HOW TO GET THERE?	Line U1 - Messberg
WHAT IS IT?	It is without a doubt one of the best museums that I have ever visited. In a short summary, you can find cities and landscapes in miniature. Have fun!
SUGGESTIONS / INTERNET	The prices can be found on the website. It is recommended to book in advance as it is a very busy place: https://www.miniatur-wunderland.com/

	# CHILE HAUS "BUILDING" ## (+/- 10 minutes)
LOCATION / MAP	
HOW TO GET THERE?	Line U1 - Messberg
WHAT IS IT?	The famous "Chilehaus" was also, together with the "Speicherstadt" declared a World Heritage Site in 2015. When Chile exported nitrate in the 1870s, the German trader Henry Sloman made a fortune with it. Therefore, he decided to build this building in commemoration of Chile. It looks like the bow of a ship on one side and today mainly has offices, but also shops.
SUGGESTIONS / INTERNET	https://www.hamburg.com/architecture/12622390/chilehaus/
FOOD OR DRINKS?	Since Turkish immigration to Germany, after the end of the Second World War has been very important – also their gastronomy has had great influence. The restaurant "Bona´me" (https://www.bona-me.de/) is an excellent alternative for those who want to try something different. The Turkish food is very delicious and prices are relatively low. Try this new concept where you order food directly from the chefs.

DAY 2 – WATER & NIGHTLIFE

	EPPENDORF / CANALS "NEIGHBORHOOD" (+/- 20 minutes)
LOCATION / MAP	
HOW TO GET THERE?	Line U3 - Eppendorfer Baum or Hoheluftbrücke
WHAT IS IT?	Eppendorf is mainly a residential area of the upper and upper middle class. There are very nice older buildings and beautiful canals, parks, but also many cafes, restaurants, shops, etc. It is a very nice place to go for a little walk.
SUGGESTIONS / INTERNET	https://www.hamburg.com/residents/neighbourhoods/12950598/eppendorf/
FOOD OR DRINKS?	The "Café & Bar Celona" is an "All you can eat" style restaurant, that offers an excellent breakfast buffet. But you can also order à la carte have lunch, dinner, and even come later to enjoy some good drinks. Additionally they have a beautiful decoration!

AUSSENALSTER LAKE
(+/- 30 minutes)

LOCATION / MAP	
HOW TO GET THERE?	Line U1 – Hallerstrasse
WHAT IS IT?	The "Aussenalster" is the larger "lake" of the both (we went to the Binnenalster yesterday). In summer you can see a lot of people sailing, on canoes and small boats on the water. And in the park there are usually many running, cycling or walking.
SUGGESTIONS / INTERNET	http://alster-cliff.de/site/
FOOD OR DRINKS?	The Alstercliff is a waterfront restaurant / bar with a spectacular view. The prices are a bit higher. Instead of spending much money on an expensive meal, we recommend only a short stay having an espresso / beer to enjoy the view.

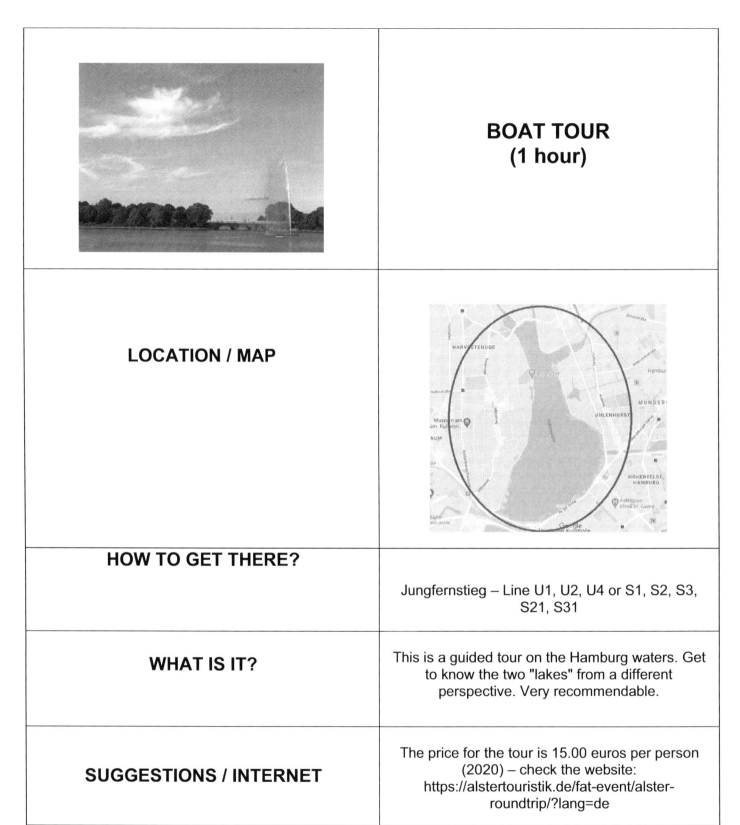

	BOAT TOUR **(1 hour)**
LOCATION / MAP	
HOW TO GET THERE?	Jungfernstieg – Line U1, U2, U4 or S1, S2, S3, S21, S31
WHAT IS IT?	This is a guided tour on the Hamburg waters. Get to know the two "lakes" from a different perspective. Very recommendable.
SUGGESTIONS / INTERNET	The price for the tour is 15.00 euros per person (2020) – check the website: https://alstertouristik.de/fat-event/alster-roundtrip/?lang=de

	**ELBSTRAND "BEACH"** **(+/- 30 minutes)**
LOCATION / MAP	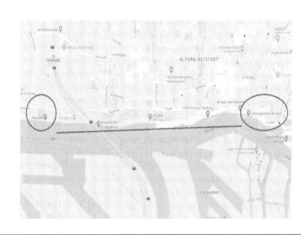
HOW TO GET THERE?	From Landungsbrücken you can get there by ferry in about 15-20 minutes.
WHAT IS IT?	The famous and very popular "Elbstrand" is right in front of the port. Although the water could be cleaner for swimming, it is a very entertaining place. Many people come (not only on Weekends) for a picnic, to do sunbathing, beach sports or just to drink a beer and enjoy the view.
SUGGESTIONS / INTERNET	https://www.hamburg.de/sehenswuerdigkeiten-am-wasser/9763364/elbstrand-hamburg/
FOOD OR DRINKS?	Strandperle is an excellent place to sit at a table (in the sand) with a beer while watching ships passing by.

	STERNSCHANZE "NEIGHBORHOOD" **(1-2 hours)**
LOCATION / MAP	
HOW TO GET THERE?	Lines U3/S11/S21/S31 - Sternschanze or line U3 Feldstrasse
WHAT IS IT ?	It is one of the most popular neighborhoods for going out. It has a large selection of small restaurants and bars with a unique atmosphere and people from all over the world. But you can also go just for a coffee during the day or even for breakfast. There are also several small shops.
SUGGESTIONS / INTERNET	https://www.hamburg.com/dine-and-drink/bars-pubs/by-location/sternschanze/
FOOD OR DRINKS?	OMAS APOTHEKE is a great pub at the entrance of the neighborhoods with a good atmosphere and very affordable prices. Not just for a beer, but also to eat something. In the winter you should better arrive early to find a table (there is no seating outside). KATZE is a very cool bar with a great atmosphere which is almost always full. The drinks are of excellent quality. The same rule as above: Arrive early, especially on Fridays or Saturdays, around 6 p.m.

	**REEPERBAHN / ST. PAULI** **"NEIGHBORHOOD"** **(1-2 hours)**
LOCATION / MAP	
HOW TO GET THERE?	Line U3 - St. Pauli or lines S1/S2/S3/S21/S31 Reeperbahn
WHAT IS IT?	A unique sector of Hamburg, also unique in Germany. It is a long street with lots of clubs, bars, restaurants and prostitutes. That's right, don't be surprised to see lots of prostitutes, sex shops and red lights in this neighborhood. Especially on Fridays and Saturdays you can see many people, locals and tourists on the street and in the area, and thats until the early hours of the following day.
SUGGESTIONS / INTERNET	https://www.hamburg.com/must-sees/11747384/reeperbahn/
FOOD OR DRINKS?	There are many options here. But "STRAND PAULI" is a very special and nice beach bar located directly in front of the harbor. Even if the prices May be a little bit higher, the atmosphere is always very good and totally worth it. They also have good food. From the Reeperbahn you walk down about 10 minutes towards the Elbe river. It is not difficult to find.

DAY 3 – TOWARDS THE WEST OF THE CITY

	FISH MARKET **(At least 1 hour)**
LOCATION / MAP	
HOW TO GET THERE?	You take the ferry from the "Landungsbrücken" the direction to the West - you get off at the first station with the same Name "Altona fish market". Alternatively, you can take the S-Bahn to "Königstraße" or "Reeperbahn" and then walk for about 10 minutes.
WHAT IS IT?	It is the most important and largest market in the whole city. It is a tourist attraction where you can not only buy fish, but also fruits, vegetables, almost everything you can think of. This fish market starts every Sunday at 5:00 a.m. (Summer) and 7:00 a.m. (winter) in the morning. Some go straight after partying, others get up very early. We leave it up to you.
SUGGESTIONS / INTERNET	https://www.guiadealemania.com/fischmarkt-de-hamburgo/
FOOD OR DRINKS?	A Fischbrötchen, fish in a bread, is very typical (see photo above). You should definitely try it before you leave town.

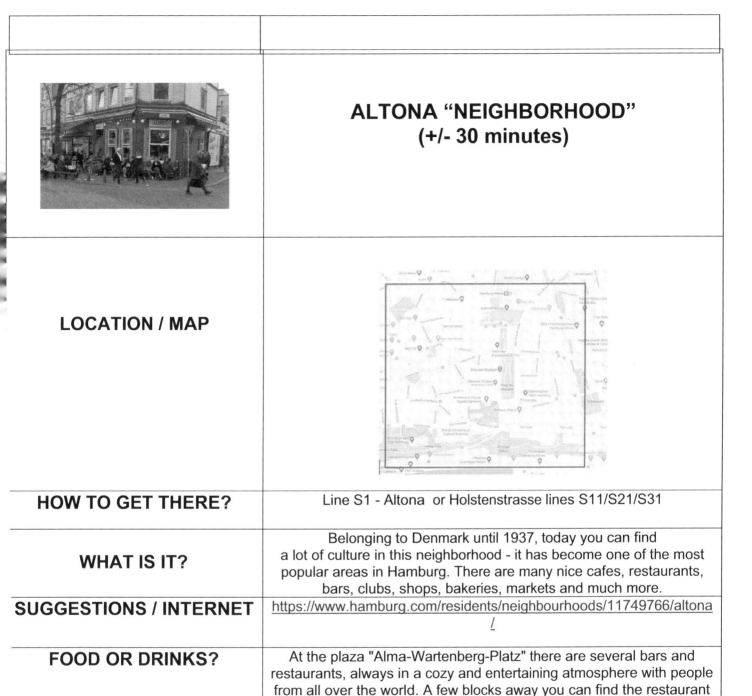

	ALTONA "NEIGHBORHOOD" **(+/- 30 minutes)**
LOCATION / MAP	
HOW TO GET THERE?	Line S1 - Altona or Holstenstrasse lines S11/S21/S31
WHAT IS IT?	Belonging to Denmark until 1937, today you can find a lot of culture in this neighborhood - it has become one of the most popular areas in Hamburg. There are many nice cafes, restaurants, bars, clubs, shops, bakeries, markets and much more.
SUGGESTIONS / INTERNET	https://www.hamburg.com/residents/neighbourhoods/11749766/altona/
FOOD OR DRINKS?	At the plaza "Alma-Wartenberg-Platz" there are several bars and restaurants, always in a cozy and entertaining atmosphere with people from all over the world. A few blocks away you can find the restaurant "CafeReise Bar". It has excellent food and drinks at low prices. Especially in summer it's great to sit outside and watch people pass by on this busy street.

	# BLANKENESE / TREPPENVIERTEL ## (+/- 35 minutes)
LOCATION / MAP	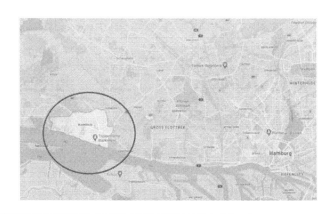
HOW TO GET THERE?	Lines S1/S11 - Blankenese
WHAT IS IT?	Blankenese is a small relaxing town on the outskirts of Hamburg. The beautiful houses on the slopes offer a great view over the river and the passing ships. There is also the famous "stairs district" where you can walk around the little hills and expect small surprises. Apart from seeing amazingly nice properties, you will find small cafes, shops and restaurants. Don't be shy and say hello to the neighbors. People are very friendly.
SUGGESTIONS / INTERNET	https://www.hamburg.com/residents/neighbourhoods/11750234/blankenese/
FOOD OR DRINKS?	The FISCHclub Blankenese is right on the water, where you might want to enjoy a delicious plate of local fish and a glass of white wine, while the ships pass by on the Elbe. Given that this restaurant is located in rather fancy and wealthy Blankenese, the prices are totally accessible for anyone. Totally worth it.

	**PLANTEN UN BLOMEN "PARK"** **(+/- 25 minutes)**
LOCATION / MAP	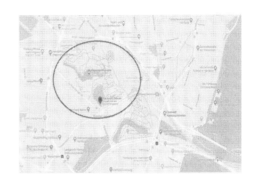
HOW TO GET THERE?	Line U1 - Stephansplatz
WHAT IS IT?	It is a very nice, huge park in the heart of the city. At the same time, you feel that you are on the countryside. It is perfect for a walk, run or just to relax. There are even large public chairs. Have a seat and enjoy !
SUGGESTIONS / INTERNET	https://plantenunblomen.hamburg.de/
FOOD OR DRINKS?	KLIMPERKISTE is a little hidden pub with a unique and very pleasant atmosphere. The prices are very affordable, and there is not only good beer but also good pub food. Cheers! The HOFBRÄUHAUS is more touristy and expensive, but it's a great place to gather with a bigger group of friend or to watch a football game. It is very big and there are always a lot of people. This is sort of an "Oktoberfest" restaurant / bar with typical Bavarian food and beer. Why not?

	**LANGE REIHE "NEIGHBORHOOD" (+/- 20 minutes)**
LOCATION / MAP	
HOW TO GET THERE?	Line U1 - Lohmühlenstrasse
WHAT IS IT?	This is a little hidden district behind the main train station full of bars, restaurants, cafes and shops. Known as the "gay / lesbian" district, you come across a very cosmopolitan atmosphere with food/drinks at fairly low prices. Try it out!
SUGGESTIONS / INTERNET	https://www.hamburg.com/residents/neighbourhoods/11750518/st-georg/
FOOD OR DRINKS?	The FRAU MÖLLER is a restaurant / bar with a very cozy atmosphere. It's perfect for a beer, but there is also excellent typical German food - also at very affordable prices.

¿GOT EVEN MORE TIME IN HAMBURG?

Of course there is even much more to do / see in Hamburg. Unfortunately many people just come for the weekend or maybe 3 days. For those, who can / want to stay longer, the ones who will live in Hamburg or who will be travelling here more often, we have this last section with further secrets of the German port city. Be prepared!

	EIMSBÜTTEL "NEIGHBORHOOD" **(+/- 20 minutes)**
LOCATION / MAP	
HOW TO GET THERE?	Line U2 - Osterstrasse or Lutterothstrasse
WHAT IS IT?	It is a very nice residential area similar to Eppendorf, but a bit further outside the city and more quiet. It is middle and upper middle class and you can also find very nice old houses and buildings. It is known for its various green areas, parks, cafes, restaurants, bars and shops. Come and go for a walk!
SUGGESTIONS / INTERNET	https://www.hamburg.com/residents/neighbourhoods/11750322/eimsbuettel/
FOOD OR DRINKS?	The "Café im Park" is literally a café in the beautiful and quiet "Eimsbüttler Park". It's the perfect place to have a coffee or beer and watch people go by. Very relaxing view. One of my favorite places, not touristy.

KAYAK RENTAL DORNHEIM
(1-2 hours)

LOCATION / MAP 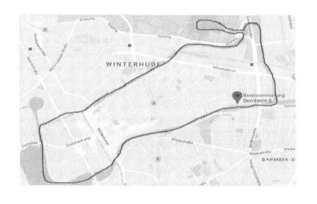	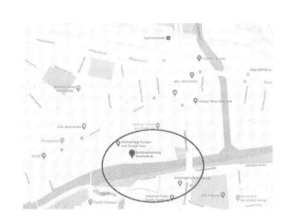
HOW TO GET THERE?	Line U3 - Saarlandstrasse
WHAT IS IT?	Here you can rent kayaks/little boats with different options. Depending on the number of people, we recommend renting a kayak to start with. As shown in the map above, you can even go kayaking to the "Aussenalster", the larger "lake". You paddle through very small canals and nice surroundings. On a sunny day, it is recommended to come early as the place might run out of kayaks. It is perfect for those who want to get to know the city in a different way, and experience the magic of the canals. There are even
SUGGESTIONS / INTERNET	https://www.bootsvermietung-dornheim.de/
FOOD OR DRINKS?	At the same place there is a restaurant "Zur Gondel", where you can sit by the water and watch people passing by on kayaks. Breakfast is a great option – prices are fairly low.

	# UNIVERSITY DISTRICT / GRINDEL ## (+/- 20 minutes)
LOCATION / MAP	
HOW TO GET THERE?	Close to train station Dammtor
WHAT IS IT?	The University of Hamburg is located here. It is a very nice cosmopolitan area with lots of parks, but also cheap cafes, restaurants and bars (made for students). There is also a colony of Jews here.
SUGGESTIONS / INTERNET	http://grindel.de/viertel/
FOOD OR DRINKS?	DOWN UNDER is an Australian pub with a great atmosphere. A few waiters are native English speakers. There is good beer and the food is delicious. The prices, compared to other places in Hamburg, are quite low. The Pony Bar is a café that turns into a bar at night. It is somewhat alternative, also has special chairs, but in general it is a nice place and interesting to see this other side of Hamburg.

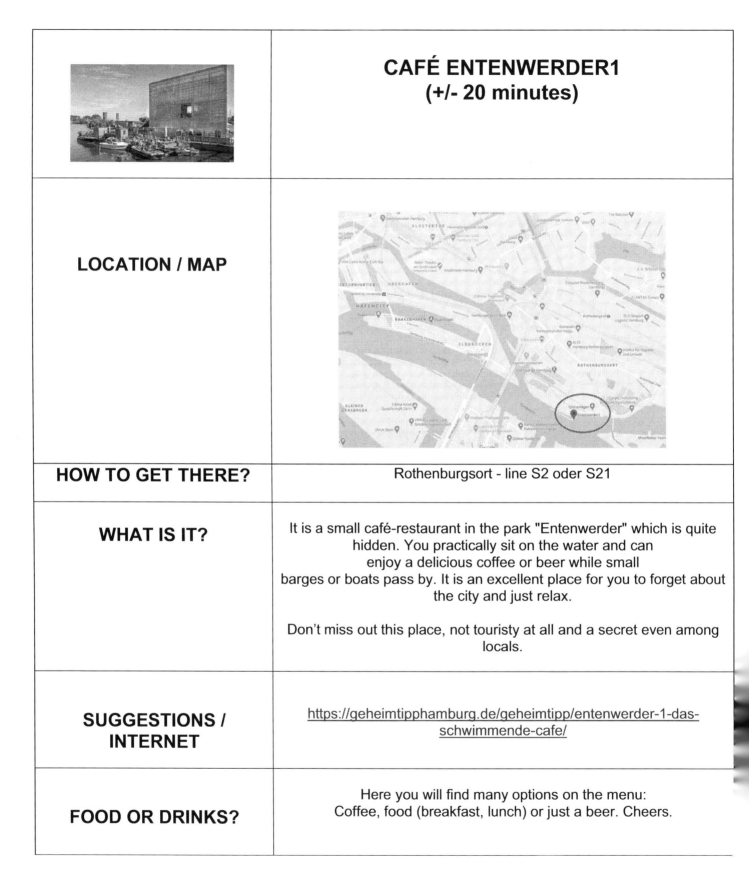	**CAFÉ ENTENWERDER1** **(+/- 20 minutes)**
LOCATION / MAP	
HOW TO GET THERE?	Rothenburgsort - line S2 oder S21
WHAT IS IT?	It is a small café-restaurant in the park "Entenwerder" which is quite hidden. You practically sit on the water and can enjoy a delicious coffee or beer while small barges or boats pass by. It is an excellent place for you to forget about the city and just relax. Don't miss out this place, not touristy at all and a secret even among locals.
SUGGESTIONS / INTERNET	https://geheimtipphamburg.de/geheimtipp/entenwerder-1-das-schwimmende-cafe/
FOOD OR DRINKS?	Here you will find many options on the menu: Coffee, food (breakfast, lunch) or just a beer. Cheers.

THANKS VERY MUCH

First of all, I would like to thank the city of Hamburg itself, because I felt so comfortable there so quickly. The many beautiful parks, canals, that awesome cosmopolitan atmosphere everywhere, all those entertaining neighborhoods with the countless cafes, restaurants, bars, etc. made me feel at home immediately.

I would also like to thank everyone who was there during my stay in Hamburg and part of my life. Some friends I already knew from Chile, but I luckily also made new friendships during my stay. Thanks also to great colleagues from work, from university, and even from a Facebook group with whom we played soccer once a week. Great times.

Thank you, I will never forget my time in Hamburg which will always stay in my heart.

Thank you, reader, for purchasing this guidebook and I sincerely hope very much that it was helpful for your visit to Hamburg. Please feel free to contact me over Instagram or Youtube directly, if you have any other further question about the city.

I hope you could/will visit as many places as possible and have a lot of fun in this amazing city. Thank you!

Printed in Great Britain
by Amazon

84834673R00021